# Towards The Lilacs

Drishti Lohiya

BookLeaf
Publishing
India | USA | UK

Made with ❤ on the BookLeaf Publishing Platform
www.bookleafpub.in
www.bookleafpub.com

# Dedication

*To all the people,*
*who have shaped me,*
*into the person i am...*

# Preface

**Playlist for my Book**
**(Music is my forte)**
**(Playlist available on Apple Music/ Spotify**
**as "towards the lilacs" by drishti)**


"Kehne laga" by Rushil Aswal

"Army Dreamers" by Kate Bush

"There is a light that never goes out" by The Smiths

"Jahan Mein Aisa Kaun hai" by Asha Bhosle

"I Love You So" by The Walters

"Out Of My League" by Fitz and The Tantrums

"End Of Beginning" by Djo

"hearts never break" by When Chai Met Toast

"be gentle with me" by yeaow

"Sailor Song" by Gigi Perez

"Abhi Na Jao Chhod Kar" by Asha Bhosle & Mohd.
Rafi

"Home" by Edith Whiskers

"I Bet on Loosing Dogs" by Mitski

"My Love Mine All Mine" by Mitski

"Saiyyan" by Kailash Kher

"Ye Tune Kya Kiya" by Pritam & Javed Bashir

"Ava" by Famy

"CO2" by Prateek Kuhad

"Tum Jab Paas" by Prateek Kuhad
and more...

Prateek Kuhad, Anuv Jain, Alec Bejamin, Lana Del Ray,
Cigerattes After Sex, Coldplay, AUR & The Local Train
are some singers/bands who have my heart.

# Acknowledgements

This book is a dream i saw in a very distant future, which BookLeaf has made a reality at the mere age of 18.

I started writing poetry not even 2 years ago, there are people i cannot even name, who have made me the person i am today. Thank you, thank you cause without you i wouldn't even have a muse to write on.

Delightfully so my family, my biggest supporter who always gave me everything without even ever questioning once, trusting me with everything. You're my lovely soul ma papa, you're my love Lakshi and Atharv.

Also, thank you to my lovely friend Himangi Singhal for listening to my poems, my rants and all of my stupid, weird life philosophy, listening to me for hours without getting bored or judging me.

Also, to the ones, who always supported me no matter my actions or words. Thank you, from all my heart, i don't know how i would ever be able to reach the gratitude my heart has for you.

I would also like to thank each and every person who has ever told me, how lovely i write or how they like my creative, everyone who has supported me even in my dumbness, Mahi Malik - for always hyping me up, Shreya Jain - for listening to my weird talks, Zuha Siddique - for always supporting me, Somya Katyayan - for all the years you've been by my side and Khushi - for making me smile in the worst of times.

And everyone who listened to my poems even when tired. And at last, I wish to thank the past me, the me who always dwells on even in the darkest parts of her life, who never gives up, never stops trying, no matter what she had to face, she never backed down, even when tired she strives, even if not showing her best. The only thing that matters is that she, always shows up. Thank you drishti, I'm proud of you.

# My Realm

A realm so far away,
mortality makes no appearance.
in the sadness of my tranquility
I drown in darkness.
I want to be away
where no soul can reach
where no cracks of sadness can seep.
through and through,
the calmness will surround
with my soul
knowing no bounds.

but this sadness of a place,
we continue to survive in.
where is the oceans to happiness,
they said we would dive in.

I will create a realm
oh so far away,
where peace will reach you
hold you so close
like the rain hold the air
the ground it seeps to.
*"my baby"* peace will call you

i will rest assured,
i will be safe
cause in a realm that far away
no soul will appear.

I want the light to leave me alone too,
i shall stay there to never return
to have a place so calm
where I will rule, with nothing to rule over.

in the darkness we will make a home,
hang lights so dull like a snowy winter noon.

no stress, no pressure, no chase I will have,
i will forget dates exist
or even that there are labs.

I will live everyday like there were no more to come
and in the darkness
we will create our light,
that will lead us,
to wherever, the destination, is to arrive.

# After i kill myself

but i fear, i fear,
what if the morning after I kill myself
i am not gone.
what if i have to stay and watch.
what if i stand in a corner watching
never visible and never to be touched.

i fear, what if the morning after I kill myself,
i watch my parents absorb the call of my death.
i watch the sun rise but do not feel it.
i listen to the echoes of laughter i had ever been a reason
of,
i listen to the sobs that thunder.

I fear, i fear the morning after i kill myself,
what if i watch my sister sitting on her bedroom floor,
trying desperately to believe i still existed.
my brother who once hugged me randomly
loses the love, with a fear of touch.
I fear, i fear the morning after i kill myself
i will stand at the feet of my body,
asking her the question of why.
trying my hardest to get some sense into her silent mind
but i fear the wanting of that

silent mind could become the reason of my screaming
soul.

and i fear, i fear what if the morning after i kill myself,
all i would want, would be to unkill myself,
but i won't be able to finish what I started.

# Mirage

between the tall trees i stood,
as the wind blew my hair away
under the shadows of high clouds i saw,
a blurry image so far away
oh so far away a mirage i saw,
baffled in thoughts, of silence,
of peace, *of home.*

the mirage walked towards me,
as slowly as the sun moves in the sky
as the moon hides behind the clouds.

the mirage, a blurred shadow
gracefully admired the pathway to my heart
as it let down all the walls it
built around for disguise in the calm.

the mirage as in the depths of
the surface of the ocean so far,
eyes, I saw, so pretty and calm
even dandelions could not compete their charm.
A smile, that lit up the
whole soul alive and apart.

I could not fathom,
the existence of beauty such kind.
even under the trees I stood,
bowed down as the wind slowly
let their breath alive.

A calm question came to the violence,
*"what is your name,*
 *the one so elegant yet fierce in the silence?"*

as the mirage stood taller
than I had reconciled,
a white beauty followed
close behind.

at the back of the beauty
hung a fiery red saddle,
an armour kept safely beside.

The pathway to my heart
had flowers cherishing their beauty.
at the end of the path, a door so carved,
with a lock, there was no key made for in this time.

standing under the tree so tall
he held out his hand to mine.
that is when the wave of fear

took a rise, so fierce and violet at all times.

scared, I was for the first of times,
there had been a flower in a land so dry.

another smile was formed on the
face of the mirage I felt so close to,
for the mirage to be mine.

a hand on my shoulder was
kept with a smile.
a whisper of the loveliest voice
that I had ever had the chance to unwind,
*"don't worry love,*
*I will keep you safe for all of my lifetime."*

that is when the fear *was scared,*
It left with none left behind.

peace came to me,
from a world, I had never
considered mine.

that is when I knew,
In all these years, kept aside
At last,
the wait eternity had given.

that is when I knew,
*my knight had arrived.*

# To the boy I could never love

to the boy i could never love,
there is a light in your eyes that could never be kept
aside,
shining with hope at all times.

to the boy i could never love,
the weight of your heart is the purest someone could
wish for,
you hand it to me with all the delicacy you have,
every day and every night.

to the boy i could never love,
every time there's a tear glittering in my eyes,
its yours that trickles down
the path mine wasn't let to.
the burden of your heart is so innocent,
with everything you try.

to the boy i could never love,
it is a tragedy the strings of our hearts were
never meant to be intertwined,
and i know it is for me to decide,
that someday your hope might come alive.

but as i watch you,
pouring your soul into not letting my tears come to life,
it is you that has to decide,
the sound of your love shattering every day and night,
is something that kills me from the inside.

to the boy i could never love,
as I watch you walk away carrying
*a heart I could never hold,*
realise the cruelest thing i ever did
was to *let you believe i could.*

# Smile

I don't know how it began,
but my layers of armour had been bought down.
the walls I built around my heart had been disintegrated
the sword used to tear souls apart from self,
had been kept away in disguise.
*the sheath covering my knife,*
*had been painted with flowers.*

I don't know how it began,
but it never used to feel safe, protected.
was he aware?
of how his mesmerising soul had been calming mine,
of how his smile had started to feel protective,
of how his embracement felt like home.

I don't know how it began,
but if someone would ask me to talk about love.
I would talk about him.
If death would grant me one wish before the end,
I would ask to see him smile,
to reach the end in his arms.

I don't know how it began,
but now it's fearful, fearful to imagine a life

without his smile.
At the darkest of nights, I ask myself,
 *"was I even alive, before I saw you smile?"*

I don't know how it began,
but now my soul had been bewitched, divided.
I never would've imagined myself feeling so much
delighted.
I ask of you to pull me closer and let me dive
into your eyes, there's a million stories to recite.

I don't know how it began,
but now if someone would question my want
to be with you forever,
I would purely recite,
*"with him, I'd want forever to last longer."*

# Mountain

there no emotions lined up at my feet today,
as i lay in bed tears make their way guided by light
outside,
though none makes it to the destination they are to
arrive
cause she screams and screams until she buries herself
alive.

there is a light, of different kind,
where maybe she could shine. maybe she
doesn't have to be desperate to feel alive.
no life no love no chase she has,
just her and her empty dreams that lie.

wanted to be a pretty girl full of surprise,
until she realised they never really liked such price.
wanted to be pretty, pretty for him to see.
but as she thinks maybe he doesn't find her so much in
life.

*why do you do this to yourself love?*
*don't you want to be happy and smile?*
if so, you need to let go of the hand you're trying so
desperately to hold and trying to hide.

let go of those who aren't enough to be a reason of your
smile.

and here she stands now, looks at you with
all the tears buried and the nights spent crying,
wish she were enough, enough for you to shine.
yet its her who always tried to ask the birds
to learn a song which makes that lil child in you smile.

so here we stand, both at the edge
*of a mountain we built ourselves,*
choosing whether to jump or live at the
high they are never meant to survive.

# in a wrecked heart

delicacy in my eyes,
i saw for myself
for the first of times
i smiled in a while.

you look so pretty with
those golden brown eyes
the flower shop
I never meant to visit,
might become the one,
I come back in all of the riddle.

I closed my eyes that night
floated in the fields of dandelions
asked myself a question that shouldn't
have waited this long to arrive,
*"was I even alive, before I saw you smile?"*

*"coffee or books?"* you ask a random light.
*"why not both, with a view to delight?"*
and there it began, the hope in a wrecked heart,
the blink on a dark night,
the blueness in those grey clouded skies.

the seconds they passed,
the days delight,
seasons changed with the look in your eyes.

*"I've never fell this hard for someone before."*
is randomly said when our arms collide.
you hold me so close in the most empty nights.
*"I'm scared"* he said whilst
I hide in a shoulder that feels mine.
*"why?"* you ask with a
look of concern in your eyes.

*"of losing you"*
these words said can never reconcile.
*"you'll never lose me"*
you say with the softest of smiles.

my silent sobs thunder through the
walls of my heart.
it's not that I didn't want to let you go,
but you left when everything felt safer inside.

Initiation was mine, I was crying all nights.
so over the walls of your house
thundering as you let the screams out one time.
love is the prettiest thing,
but getting ugly it destroys the within.

so maybe it's good you left,
you smile a lot more besides.
and maybe this time,
looking in the mirror, I'll ask myself
*"was I even alive, before I saw you smile?"*

# thee is me

you hide it so right,
coated in layers of delight
the smiles never meant
the eyes never hurt
the smile that forever fades
the love that forever unhinges
i hate you, i'm scared of you
the world is better without you
the skies seem happier when you're not under it
the light, the blushes, the clouds, the stars are better
without you
the hatred has consumed thee
the guilt will destroy you.

~ talk to yourself like you talk of others,
 and you shall realise how
 the shadow in the mirror deserves
 a thousand more smiles.

# time

there was a time I could not have smiled,
there was a time my eyes held no
words like that of a dying life,
this time was the worst with all
the others combine.

but then, eyes beautiful as rosemary,
smile, lovely as the shore and
laughs with the melody I could listen to
for hours, never needing a pause they called for every
once in a while.

I found a home I had never imagined
could be mine.
the tales of love were told in every
beauty you could find,
in every song you could recite.
love is a beautiful thing, my love
but also a *knife twisted yourself* deeper inside.

there is a silence so fast,
the meaning fades somewhere never found alive.
In the corners of places light can
never reach,

I'll build a home.
and maybe I would pray every night
asking for the light to reach me sometime.

but it never will,
cause i built a home in the place
light never finds.

Isn't that what we always wish for?
something not possible,
something that never had a meaning.
*why?* they ask
cause they build a home where no light
can reach ever to feel alive.

so i shift, places,
homes, hearts,
eyes and finally mirrors.

i change my mirrors,
they show me the lovely parts of
myself i never saw.

this journey goes to places i never
knew could exist in my life,
how lovely of a home i will
build in a place lit so

beautifully inside.

and then there will be a time,
where i will forevermore smile,
and where my eyes will hold a million stores to recite.

# a place

i told the moon that night,
how i wish the stars would guide,
me to a place where heavens arrive,
where loneliness is only a word to describe,
where knives are not bled into your life.

even the heavens,
smiled at my silly mind.
*i've told you a million times,*
*there is no place,*
*where melancholy is not alive.*
said the moon with no intention to unwind.

a place where shadows have a life
and know no place to be bind.

someday,
this silly little mind will find,
the world is what it feels like,
to be the light,
that never had a dark place to shine.

# leave behind

A destiny needs to be reached,
way life moves
it doesn't matter anymore,
for good or worse.
My mind explodes with all the small pieces left.
Hatred consumes the last living cell.
With your eyes on me,
life takes no turn.
only if now,
you'll understand,
love lasts if hurt ends.
*this or that*, one will be hurt
no more ways to get out alive.
Either a bullet passes through this head of mine,
leaving all this guilt behind.
life will seem so calm then,
with no brokenness to look at.

You will be gone, forgive love
life lasts if acceptance achieve
the dumbest deeds in life.

Forgive me soul, you are not at fault
Leave all this wreck behind.

# i still want you.

you killed the child in me,
and I still want you.
you will never understand me,
and I still want you.
you put a knife of tears in my throat
i will never be able to speak,
and I still want you.
you made me hate the things I loved,
and I still want you.
you made me go friendless,
completely unsocial,
and I still want you.
you made me doubt everything about myself,
and I still want you.
you made me change when I had
never even discovered myself,
and I still want you.
you hurt me in ways I never knew I could be hurt,
and I still want you.
you called me what-not,
and I still want you.

you are the knife I turned inside myself,
you are the walls I bound myself into,

you are the ocean I drown in,
you are the reason my heart beats yet it breaks.
and I still want you.

for there will be a day,
and there is a day i look back at,
where all i wanted was you.
you, you and you.
as today i stand here,
at the feet of the corpse you created.
i don't even scream some sense into her mind.

cause it is time,
that will show,
how love is sometimes only
a reality to plough.

and it will be time to show,
that one day,
i will want everything,
but you.

# whisper

the silence in my eyes would speak stories
if someone would listen,
the delight, the gloomy,
all taken with the eyes of a corpse.
if one would listen,
i will not talk,
if one would try to read those stories,
my eyes will be closed.
none will know, the oceans i create.
none will know the beauty i leave.
So do not dare to try,
even if my soul screams with a cry.
the words never able to come out,
reaching the tongue and
being buried alive.
they can try, though none will,
to have me "talk about it"
but what will i say?
mortality is the reason i will not face them.
i will turn and return to the dark home
i built with gloomy lights.
rather be alone and dark,
than be broken by these mortals,
pretending to be fine.

# "free"

what if i told you, there is a world
where you smile with no fear of knife
which is held so tight.

what if i told you, there is a world
carved out, for a girl with a
mind so bright, A world for
her brilliance to be mastered with no
bounds she knows of.

They had once asked her,
*"what do you want to be when you grow up?"*
only one word had screamed to shatter the light,
a thunder had roared though her heart,
burning her being alive,
*"free"*
*"i wish to be free...*
        *when i grow up"*

# not mine

your heart will wreck and burn but
find a way to sew,
your soul will love and hate but
find a way to smile within chaos
you seem like the prettiest existence one could
dream of, yet it was never meant for my heart to scream
of
your name seems lovely yet not made for my tongue
sometimes
you are my home, my love my haven yet your soul
deserves more
i am not yours, you light the world alight
where i am the darkness consuming it.
i should have left when you screamed through my head.
i should have gone when your eyes were wet.
i do not deserve the love you foreshadow as
my soul has already given up on any blueness you
create.
grey and grey is all i see.
grey and grey is all there is for me.

~ why did it had to be me,
for your soul to kill and scream?

# that girl

no words i find,
to thread these tears into,
silence, perhaps a silence so vast
blur are the bounds i created.

left all mortals in the past
today its so empty
i hear my own echoes
thundering through my own heart

my echoes,
she says,
*"utmost pride bubbles in my soul,
as you stand silently alone."*

*"you learn from the dark times"*
they had told her,
but her question remained forever
with a spark
*never did i want to learn,*
*never did i wished to be strong,*
*love, peace and warmth.*

a warmth so lovely,

peace bled through her eyes
a love so pure,
even a girl possessor of love,
finds beautifully immense.

ache in her soul
cuts in her throat
she gave her heart away.
once in a beautiful moon,
she'll come to realise,
knowing *her heart is to be
given, to her own soul.*

# beauty

i wish your eyes were a little less talkative,
a little less pretty and a little less dreamy.
at dark nights i wonder if there were ever to be a time,
where your eyes would look into mine.
free of will, walking down the path i shall not cross,
through forests of dreamy days
blossoms and oaks,
through fields of golden light
through trails of broken hearts
under the stars,
to a place your smiles were mine.
if i fell asleep maybe i will reach,
a place where eternity was not
just for memories combined.

he slow fall,
the gloomy night,
the pretty sky,
your pure brown eyes,
my vision blurs as the fall ascends,
still falling, when a laughter rings in my head.
still falling, when a smile appears.
still falling, with closed eyes as i smile to me in that
night.

all my dreams desires and hopes were fulfilled,
so pretty i find this world,
will i ever find that beauty to reside in me atleast once in
a lifetime?

# november

maybe november is the month of lovers,
the month of someone who gives it all
the month of people who smiled at the
saddest parts.

maybe november is the month
of fallen trees,
the month of people who broke
their own heart,
the month of the ones who hope
for even that lightest chance.

but what if november,
was never mine?
i was trying so hard to rise and shine,
when all it bought me was tears and
smiles with sadness buried alive?

# hidden within

as december ends and the year begins to cease,
i think and thank that sulky girl in me,
you pause and break and smile still,
all the while as you walk with pride and shame
combined,
you fall and fall into an endless blur
when at the end you fall more down and down
yet your eyes never stop seeing that light shining above
that lazy crazy girl in me
you're cute and dumb when you cry like a child
easy on you i will go not,
no matter how hard it gets for you
you will smile and move with me
even when you wanna kill me from within
i will let you be the one you desire
and you will make me the one they do not believe you to
be.
that lazy silly girl in me,
you are so pure, keep trust in me
let the universe hold your pain
that endless stream of sinking thoughts
don't let them be the part of your drought
and even when drought arrives,
let the land be the memoir of your tears and it shall

thrive.
i know we will make it out of this grassland,
i know the world awaits a self made princess,
your smile and eyes, your hopes and lies,
with everything in me, just remember the one thing
no one will tell you with pure honesty,
*it is you, you have to look within.*
and the answer lies there, hidden somewhere
for you to close your pretty eyes and find at the right
time.

# a tale never told.

Maybe i was meant to be broken,
maybe the child five years ago,
already had a chance.
maybe I was supposed to it all,
to stand here and smile.
to tell you, it was not that hard.

but it was, I will not lie,
the nights passed were covered in the dark.
a storm raging towards the shore,
yet it would be night before the lore.

they tell tales of nights passed crying,
of hands never left to hold.
let me recite one more,
of love, never enough known.

From the shadows rises a buried soul,
tonight could be his night of all.
a hope in the heart,
a light in the eyes,
steps are taken to reach the archive.

but to the destination, he never arrives,

shadows are meant to be gone,
when the light gets too high.

so maybe I'll smile waiting to be known,
and the next time that night arrives
I'll make sure to hold onto the dark
for as long as it takes for shadows
to again have a heart.

# in all the wrong places

life sat by my side, talking to me about all
the possibilities that were yet to arrive,
*"you will smile and smile without a*
 *thought crossing your mind"*
*"is that even possible when all I feel*
 *is the need to be buried alive?*
*when all the mistakes have asked to*
*be carried with me as*
*long time holds."* I ask sitting beside,
tears playing hide and seek in my eyes.

*"it was not your fault"* life says, she smiles at
me looking in my eyes as if trying to
make me crack a smile.
*"it was not your fault that*
 *all of it had been burdened on your living soul,*
*that all you had done*
*was blamed to your light shining so bright"*

*"will never be understood, will i?"* i asked her
hoping for even a tiny bit of light.
*"maybe not, but there is no need to be*
 *understood when you know yourself, and*
 *know how to make peace and love life"*

*life would be my friend,* I thought as I
looked at the words she had just told. she seems
pretty to hold out the truth even when it
feels so wrongful to, *she would be my friend.*

*maybe with life as my friend, I could once more feel
alive?*

# hope in death

My heart feels heavy right now
you seem so far.
you seem to think you're so alone
In a world full of people to love.
there is no thing I could do,
to make your heart light.
my own's sinking in the depth of a shine.
there is a stone kept my emotions
burying them to the ground.
and further and further it goes
where no light can reach
where there is no sight to see.
*you have a pretty smile,*
I tell you most nights.
you do have a pretty smile
the one I could recognise
on a stranger shore.
the smile to make my heart mold.

The smile i could recognise in death
if it were to take me away.
the smile I could hold in my soul
till I find you in the next of lives.
the smile that forms on your cheek

like the moon on a breathtaking night,
the line that forms like lightning,
through a window, so thunderous yet so calm.
your smile, I could hold forever as hope.

But the way it disappears,
when the smallest of agonies arise.
your heart depletes into the darkness,
it once buried alive.
tears that form in the sinking calmness of your eyes,
burn, as they make it down the line.
happiest I am when your soul shines,
you make me feel so alive.
I give you all the love my heart is made of combine,
to not get a smile only in return to be fine.

only if my love was enough to heal
the broken pieces of your soul.
I would be so gentle with love and care
to help the child that was once left to fall.

but it is not,
my love is not enough for you to heal,
wonder where I failed for it to be known.
I am not enough for your soul to shine bright every day
for.
makes me wonder sometimes,

if I were not there to ruin your life for all,
would you be happier?
would your soul shine every day?
If it was not me to hold you back,
would you have a better soul to mend?
and maybe it is true.

but I cannot fathom,
the thought of leaving you.
for you is all my soul ever desires.
for you is what feels to be okay.
for you is what feels to be *at home.*

*"you are my whole world"*
 you said to me last night.
*Maybe I am not the problem in your life*
it made me think.
but why is it me, my whole of love,
not enough for your soul to heal.
"beautiful things take time" they say
still, I will give you all of my soul
for as long as it takes for
shadows to again have a home.

*take your time, take it all,*
*for all of mine, is all of yours.*
*you are mine as I am yours.*

with this wreckness of a heart,
and a shadow for a soul.
with this heaviness of a calm,
and silence for a thought.
my tears trickle with no healing,
they are said to do.
your smile could heal more,
than a million tears would.

make me cry, make me laugh,
make me hurt, make me love,
I am yours too hurt,
I am yours to love.

heal yourselves,
I wish I could be enough,
you are the love,
my heart's only desire.

*you are mine, as I am yours*
*for all of mine, is all of yours.*

# "i'll be with you forever"

they say, *"I'll be with you forever."*

but i would've said, *"I am aware our lives will
not last forever, but if i love you, it will be
the purest form of me, i do not know if
we live a single life or many. but if we do,
i will love you in every life we ever live, it
does not matter if we change forms,
bodies, lives, faces. i will recognise you.,
i will recognise you by your breath, by
your voice, by you.
if i love you, i will love you in the most beautifully
destroying way possible, if i love you
i will kiss you in every moonlight night, every
wondrous day, every raining clouds and
every night before you go to sleep.
if i love you,
it won't matter."*

# in 40 years

and there he sat, fidgeting his wedding ring
as he watched the sky. time flies like
a gush of wind i think. his eyes still tell
stories that i can sink into forever. his smile
still feels like my home. his hugs feel like my
shield. he stared into the sky and said
*"lost in the clouds, can't we be?"*
*"we willsomeday be, soon enough"*
it feels too early, it feels too quick to think of
one of us leaving before the other.

it's been 40 years and we've never been apart.
40 years of beautiful memories and poetries.
i still remember the day i met him, it was one
filled with roses and rain, my teenage heart
was aching for another. had been crying for
a year, for another.

but then he looked at me from the corner of
the flower shop, and smiled.
in that moment, i knew this smile will be my home.
i questioned myself that night,
*"was i even alive, before i saw you smile?"*
but there he was, eyes beautiful as

rosemary.
and here he sits, father of our children, lover
of my teenage heart. love of my life. they
said "*don't get married just yet, it won't last*"

but here he sits staring at the clouds,
thinking of about something beautiful in his
wondrous mind. i'm thinking back my life,
my heart, my love.
the pictures on every wall of the house told
stories of our past. of us.
the coziest life i had lived, being home
with my person.

and here he sits, never afraid of the future,
he holds out his hand to mine, i reach for it
and hold it tight.
*"if one of us dies first, i wish its me. cause*
*i don't think i can ever live without you."*
i said as he repeated those words wishing
his death to be nearer than mine.